The Patron Saints of Forgiveness

THE PATRON SAINTS OF FORGIVENESS

Rev. Fr. Henry Sseriiso

THE
PATRON SAINTS
OF
FORGIVENESS

Rev. Fr. Henry Sseriiso

Leonine Publishers
Phoenix, Arizona

Nihil Obstat: Rev. Msgr. Gerard M. Lopez, STL, VG
                 Vicar General of the Diocese of San Bernardino

Imprimatur: ✠ Most Rev. Gerald R. Barnes, DD
                Bishop of the Diocese of San Bernardino
                March 2, 2011

Copyright © 2011 Henry Sseriiso

Published by Leonine Publishers LLC
Phoenix, Arizona

All rights reserved. No part of this book may be reproduced or transmitted in any form or by any means, electronic or mechanical, including photocopying, recording, or by any information storage or retrieval system now existing or to be invented, without written permission from the respective copyright holder(s), except for the inclusion of brief quotations in a review.

The Scripture citations used in this work are taken from the
HOLY BIBLE—'Catholic Companion Edition' [New American Bible],
Copyright © 2006–2007 edition by Fireside Catholic Publishing, Wichita, KS.

ISBN-13: 978-0-9843001-5-0

10 9 8 7 6 5 4 3 2

Printed in the United States of America

Cover images, clockwise from top left: St. Martin de Porres, St. Maria Goretti, St. Thomas More, Blessed Metod Dominik Trcka, the statue of St. Wenceslaus in Wenceslas Square in Prague, and St. John Gualbert.

Visit us online at www.leoninepublishers.com
For more information: info@leoninepublishers.com

Dedication

To my father, Mr. David Miiro Bijugu,
my mother, Theresa Bijugu,
and to all Consolata Missionaries.

About the Author

Father Henry Sseriiso is a Roman Catholic priest from Uganda. He currently serves at Our Lady of the Assumption Catholic Church in San Bernardino, California, in the San Bernardino Diocese, USA.

Table of Contents

INTRODUCTION   1

PART I
SAINTS WHO TEACH US TO FORGIVE   3

PART II
FORGIVENESS IN THE NEW TESTAMENT   35

PART III
REFLECTIONS ON FORGIVING ONE ANOTHER   49

    Forgiveness Promotes Life 51
    Forgiveness is More Important than Sacrifice 54
    Forgiveness Brings Healing 55
    A Command to Forgive 59
    We Are All Sinners 62
    A Forgiveness That Restores Relationships 63
    A Forgiveness that Aims at the Conversion of Others ... 65
    Some Consequences Of Unforgiveness 66

CONCLUSION   71

Introduction

Forgiveness sits at the very core of our Christian Faith and is one of the greatest challenges of Christians. When we forgive one another, we reveal Christ's presence in us, and proclaim that we are true followers of Christ. For Christ's true followers, forgiveness is not an option, but an obligation.

In this book I will present some lives of the saints, our elders in the Faith, to teach us to be forgiving people. Whenever we feel that forgiving one another is becoming difficult, we should always ask these saints to show us the way to forgiveness. Catholic saints are human beings like us, they managed to live a life of forgiveness, and can help us to do the same.

At times forgiving one another may be very difficult, but we should never abandon our efforts to forgive. Instead we should be encouraged to know that forgiveness brings joy and peace into our lives and the lives of others.

I will also offer some reflections to help us value forgiveness.

PART I

Saints Who Teach Us to Forgive

St. Maria Goretti..5
St. John Gualbert 8
St. Jane Frances de Chantal..............................9
St. Pontian and St. Hippolytus 10
St. Rita of Cascia...11
St. Martin de Porres.....................................12
St. Patrick...13
St. Stephen..14
St. Thomas More...15
Blessed Metod Dominik Trcka.........................16
St. Germaine Cousin of Pibrac.........................17
St. Agostina Pietrantoni.................................20
Blessed Miguel Pro.......................................20
St. Joseph Mukasa Balikuddembe 21
Blessed Josep Samso i Elias.............................21
Blessed Margaret of Castello............................22
St. Wenceslaus..24
Blessed Isidore Bakanja..................................25
Blessed Margaret Pole 25
Blessed Titus Brandsma..................................26
St. Antoninus 27
Blessed Lucio Martinez Mancebo and Companions..........27
St. Oliver Plunkett 28
St. Elizabeth of Portugal 29
St. Eustace White 30
St. Brice 30
St. Claudine Thevenet 31
Blessed Peter of Castelnau...............................32
St. John Grove..33

PART I

Saints Who Teach Us to Forgive

Forgiveness confirms the presence of God in our lives—the closer we move to God, the easier it becomes for us to forgive one another. The saints, being close to God, were able to grant forgiveness to others even in the most difficult situations.

St. Maria Goretti

Maria Goretti was born into poverty on October 16, 1890, in Italy. She did not have a chance to go to school, and did not know how to read or write.

From the very beginning of her life, Maria Goretti had a great love of God; she treasured her Faith. Her mother was illiterate, but a very devout Catholic. She did her best to teach her daughter the Faith.

On July 5, 1902, when Maria Goretti was only eleven years old, her life changed forever. She was alone in the house sewing her clothes, and looking after her baby sister. A 20-year-old man named Alessandro Serenelli came into her house, and threatened her with death if she did not commit the sin of impurity with him.

"I will not! It is a sin! God does not want it," Maria told Alessandro.

Alessandro attacked her, but she desperately fought to protect her purity.

"No! It is a sin! God does not want it!" She warned Alessandro repeatedly that what he wanted to do was a mortal sin, and that he would go to Hell if he persisted in it.

Alessandro stabbed her many times, leaving her almost dead, and ran away. Maria Goretti was rushed to the hospital, but it was too late. Before she died she forgave her murderer Alessandro, saying that she wanted to have him in Heaven with her. She prayed that God would also forgive Alessandro.

Alessandro was arrested and sentenced to 30 years in prison. For a long time he remained unrepentant and surly. All the years in prison and all the punishments he received could not change him. Nothing could make him realize the terrible crime he had committed, or make him repent, ask for forgiveness, and live a better moral life.

One night, Alessandro had a dream or vision of Maria Goretti lovingly offering him a bunch of beautiful flowers. This dream changed his life for good. Even in death, Maria Goretti brought forgiveness and love to her murderer. Alessandro was expecting revenge because of his crime—instead she offered him forgiveness and love. Her kindness and charity broke his heart and changed him completely. Years in prison could not alter him, but Maria's *forgiveness* brought him to repentance.

This forgiveness made Alessandro realize the sin he had committed, and start seeking ways to live a better life. When Alessandro was released from prison, he went directly to Maria Goretti's mother and asked for forgiveness.

"If my daughter forgave you, who am I to withhold forgiveness? I also forgive you," said her mother.

In this case, it was not punishment that converted the sinner, but forgiveness.

On June 24, 1950, Pope Pius XII canonized Maria Goretti. Alessandro was present at the ceremony, and cried tears of repentance and joy.

Alessandro became a lay brother of the Order of Friars Minor Capuchin, living in a monastery and working as receptionist and gardener. He died peacefully in 1970.

Alessandro left the following letter, dated May 5, 1961:

I'm nearly 80 years old. I'm about to depart. Looking back at my past, I can see that in my early youth, I chose a bad path which led me to ruin myself. My behavior was influenced by print, mass-media and bad examples which are followed by the majority of young people without even thinking. And I did the same. I was not worried. There were a lot of generous and devoted people who surrounded me, but I paid no attention to them because a violent force blinded me and pushed me toward a wrong way of life. When I was 20 years old, I committed a crime of passion. Now, that memory represents something horrible for me. Maria Goretti, now a Saint, was my good Angel, sent to me through Providence to guide and save me. I still have impressed upon my heart her words of rebuke and of pardon. She prayed for me, she interceded for her murderer. Thirty years of prison followed. If I had been of age, I would have spent all my life in prison. I accepted to be condemned because it was my own fault. Little Maria was really my light, my protectress; with her help, I behaved well during the 27 years of prison and tried to live honestly when I was again accepted among the members of society. The Brothers of St. Francis, Capuchins from Marche, welcomed me with angelic charity into their monastery as a brother, not as a servant. I've been living with their community for 24 years, and now I am serenely waiting to witness the vision of God, to hug my loved ones again, and to be next to my Guardian Angel and her dear mother, Assunta. I hope this letter that I wrote can teach others the happy lesson of avoiding evil and of always following the right path, like little children. I feel that religion with its precepts is not something we can live without, but rather it is the real comfort, the real strength in life and the only safe way in every circumstance, even the most painful ones of life. Signed, Alessandro Serenelli. [1]

Maria Goretti teaches us to forgive those who have injured us, and those who have killed our loved ones. By offering forgiveness, we liberate ourselves and at the same time we liberate those who have committed the crime.

St. John Gualbert

Saint John was born toward the end of the tenth century in Florence, Italy. John had only one brother, Hugo. John and his father were devastated when they learned that Hugo had been killed. They knew the man who had done it. Urged on by his father and by his own anger, John sought a way to avenge his brother's death. He felt that it was his responsibility.

On Good Friday of that year, John came face to face with the murderer of his brother in a narrow passageway. John drew his sword to kill him. Hugo's killer fell to his knees, crossed his arms on his chest, and begged John's forgiveness for the love of Jesus who died on the Cross. With a tremendous effort, John dropped his sword. There and then he forgave his enemy and embraced him. When

---

[1] www.mariagoretti.org/alessandrobio.htm

John came to a monastery church, he went in and knelt before the crucifix to pray. He asked God for forgiveness for his own sins. Then a miracle happened: Christ on the Cross bowed His Head. Christ seemed to be telling John that He was pleased with him for forgiving his enemy. John felt that his own sins were also forgiven. Such a change came over him that he went straight to the abbot of that monastery, and asked if he could join the monks. From then on, John Gualbert lived a holy life as a monk. John's life teaches us to forgive those who have killed our loved ones.

St. Jane Frances de Chantal

Jane was born on January 28, 1572 in Dijon, France. Her father was a devout Catholic, whose wife unfortunately died when their children were still very young. However, he managed to bring up all his children in the Christian faith. His children knew and loved their Holy Faith. When Jane was about 20 years old, she married Christopher Baron de Chantal. Jane and Christopher loved each other very much. God blessed them with six children, but sadly three died soon after their birth. Jane showed her love for God by loving her husband and children with her whole heart—theirs was a happy home.

Then, suddenly, a great tragedy fell upon that happy home. Christopher was accidentally shot and killed by a friend who had gone hunting with him.

Before he died, Christopher forgave the man who shot him, saying to the man: "Don't commit the sin of hating yourself when you have done nothing wrong."

Jane was heartbroken when her husband died. She went into a deep depression. Jane could not forgive the man who had killed her husband. She had to struggle with forgiveness for a long time. At first she tried to simply greet this man whenever she met him on the street. When she found out that she could comfortably do this, she decided to take another step. She invited him to her house on a number of occasions for a meal or a cup of tea. This brought more healing in her life.

Finally, Jane was able to tell him, "I have forgiven you."

She forgave this man so completely that she even became godmother to his child.

Saint Jane forgave the man who killed her husband. She can help us to learn to forgive people in our lives who have injured us. It was difficult for her and she struggled. She can understand our struggles toward forgiveness. We can take the steps she took to welcome back into our lives the people who have injured us.

St. Pontian and St. Hippolytus

In the year A.D. 235, Maximinus became the emperor of the Roman Empire. Almost immediately, he began to persecute the Christians. He exiled many bishops and priests to the dangerous and unhealthy mine fields in Sardinia, Italy. But it was this persecution that brought about a reconciliation between Saint Pontian and Saint Hippolytus.

Previous to the reign of Maximinus, Saint Hippolytus was a priest and a scholar in the church of Rome. He wrote many excellent works of theology and was a great teacher, but he became frustrated with Pope Saint Zephyrinus. Hippolytus felt that the pope was not quick enough to stop people who were teaching errors.

When Saint Zephyrinus was martyred in A.D. 217, he was succeeded by Saint Callistus. Hippolytus was not pleased with the choice of this new pope either. Hippolytus himself had a large following, and he agreed to their suggestion that he be appointed pope. He broke ties with the Church and became a false pope.

Meanwhile, Saint Callistus died and Saint Urban became pope. Hippolytus had been an anti-pope for eighteen years when Saint Pontian became the true pope after the death of Pope Urban I in 230. Five years later, the persecution of Christians by Maximinus began. Saint Pontian was sent into exile to Sardinia, where he stayed until his death.

Hippolytus was also arrested and sent to Sardinia. In that sad environment, Hippolytus met his enemy, Pope Pontian.

The humility of Pope Pontian touched the anti-pope. He asked the pope to forgive him and reconcile him to the Church. Pontian forgave him, and welcomed Hippolytus back. Hippolytus resigned his position as anti-pope, and accepted the Holy Father's authority. After this forgiveness, Hippolytus's anger toward the Church receded from his heart and was replaced with joy and peace.

Soon afterward both men died for their Catholic Faith. These two martyrs will forever remain witnesses of forgiveness and Christian hope.

St. Rita of Cascia

Rita was born in A.D. 1381 in Italy. Her parents were pious Catholics and raised Rita the same way. As a result, Rita became very devout at a young age.

Rita wanted to become a nun, but her parents decided that she should marry instead. In obedience to the will of her parents, Rita accepted an arranged marriage. The man they chose for Rita turned out to be rich, but quick-tempered and immoral. Saint Rita endured his insults, abuse and infidelities for eighteen years, and bore him twin sons.

Her prayers, gentleness and goodness finally won his heart. He apologized to Rita for the way he had mistreated her for so long. Rita forgave him. The man completely converted and started living a holy life. Rita was happy that now their home life would be filled with joy and happiness with God in their midst.

Rita's joy over her husband's conversion did not last long. One day, shortly after his conversion, he was murdered. Rita was shocked and heartbroken. But she forgave his killer.

Her two sons, however, were not ready to forgive the murderer of their father. Rita tried her best to make them forgive, but the twins only wanted revenge.

Eventually it was clear to Rita that her two sons were determined to avenge their father's death despite all her efforts. Rita prayed to God to take away the lives of her two sons rather than let them commit that terrible sin of murder. She knew that if they committed such a sin they would make themselves unworthy of God's Kingdom.

God heard Rita's prayer. Within a few months, both boys became seriously ill. Rita nursed them lovingly. During their illness, she continued to ask them to forgive the murderer, and to ask God's forgiveness for themselves. The twins took their saintly mother's advice, and in the end both died peacefully.

St. Martin de Porres

Martin was born in Peru on December 9, 1579. His father was a nobleman from Spain, and his black mother was a former slave, probably from Panama. Martin was dark-skinned like his mother, so he was looked upon as a slave too. He faced a lot of discrimination because of his skin color.

In those days, black people or mixed-racial people were not treated like human beings, but objects to be used and then thrown away. Martin could have grown to be a bitter person, but he did not. He forgave all those who discriminated against him and mistreated him. He was such a loving child that he was always ready to sacrifice the little he had, to share with those who were poor like him irrespective of their skin color.

He became a Dominican, and spent most of his time taking care of the sick and the poor. He was always there to help all people regardless of their color, race or status. God gave him the gift of healing, and he used this gift to help all people, even those who discriminated against him.

Martin de Porres deserves to be called the patron of Christian forgiveness. Pope John XXIII remarked at his canonization on May 6, 1962: "He excused the faults of others. He forgave the bitterest injuries...."[2]

For those who have faced racial discrimination, Saint Martin brings a message to stop blaming and start forgiving. By doing so, we can all discover the beauty in those that have hurt us, and they in turn will discover the beauty in us—and peace and joy will reign again.

St. Patrick

Saint Patrick was born in Britain in the year 387. When he was about sixteen years old, he was captured from Britain by Irish raiders and taken to Ireland. He was forced to work as a slave, taking care of the sheep in the mountains, with very little food and almost no clothing. But this did not prevent him from taking good care of the animals, even in bad weather.

After six years of slavery in Ireland, he managed to escape and went back to Britain. As a free man, his desire was to serve God, to announce the Good News. He

---

[2] Leonard Foley & Pat McCloskey, [Editors], *Saints of the Day: Lives, Lessons and Feasts*, Cincinnati: St. Anthony Messenger Press, 2003, 5th Revised Edition, p. 302.

decided to become a priest, and later was consecrated bishop.

He had a great desire to preach the gospel to the pagan people of Ireland. One day he had a dream, in which the children of Ireland were stretching out their hands to him, asking him to return to them. He took this dream to be a clear sign that Our Lord wanted him to go and announce the Good News to the Irish people.

Patrick forgave the Irish who had mistreated him for six years as a slave. To prove that he had really forgiven them, he went back to Ireland to bring them the Catholic Faith. He was happy to bring the Truth to the people who had once held him as a slave.

He set up parishes, convents and schools for the people of Ireland. He traveled from one village to another, seldom resting. He performed great penances for the people of Ireland whom he loved so much. By the time he died the whole country had become Catholic.

St. Stephen

Saint Stephen was one of the first deacons of the early Christian Church. He later became the first disciple of Christ to receive the martyr's crown.

As we read in the Acts of the Apostles (Acts. 6-7), his enemies falsely accused him of blasphemy against God and the law of Moses, and of speaking against the Temple and the Law.

As a result he was stoned to death. As he was dying he forgave those who were killing him, and he begged God not to punish his enemies for his death.

Stephen died as Jesus did: falsely accused, brought to unjust condemnation because he spoke the truth fearlessly. He died with his eyes trustfully fixed on God, and with a prayer of forgiveness on his lips. A happy death is one that finds us in the same spirit... dying with courage, total trust and forgiving love. [3]

St. Thomas More

Saint Thomas More was born on February 7, 1478, in London, England. He was a very intelligent man. He went to Oxford University where he studied law, and became a famous lawyer. Eventually King Henry VIII spotted him and appointed him to a series of important positions in his kingdom. Thomas became a great friend of King Henry VIII, and as a result, became the Lord Chancellor of England in 1529.

Thomas More's success in politics did not make him lose sight of God in his life: Thomas was a devout and active Catholic. He loved and respected the Catholic Church, and prayer was part of his daily life.

When King Henry VIII decided to divorce his wife and make himself the head of the Catholic Church in England, Thomas More naturally opposed him. Thomas therefore lost the royal favor, and in 1532, resigned from his position as Lord Chancellor of England.

Because of his opposition to the king, Thomas More was imprisoned for a long time. Eventually, he was falsely convicted of treason and sentenced to death. At first he was going to be hanged, but King Henry VIII demanded that he be beheaded instead.

Before he died, Thomas forgave all his executioners by saying,

---

[3] Leonard Foley & Pat McCloskey, [Editors], *Saints of the Day: Lives, Lessons and Feasts*, Cincinnati: St. Anthony Messenger Press, 2003, 5th Revised Edition, p. 352.

As St. Paul had persecuted St. Stephen, and yet they be now both twain holy saints in heaven, and shall continue there friends forever, so I verily trust, and shall therefore right heartily pray, that though your lordships have now here on earth been judges of my condemnation, we may yet hereafter in heaven merrily all meet together in everlasting salvation. [4]

True forgiveness demands that we bless our enemies and wish them well, and that is exactly what Saint Thomas More did.

Blessed Metod Dominik Trcka

Metod Dominik was born on July 6, 1886, in the Czech Republic. He came from a devout Catholic family, and received a good Christian education. He later joined the Congregation of the Most Holy Redeemer—the Redemptorists.

Metod Dominik was ordained a priest on July 17, 1910, and then worked as a missionary among the Greek Catholics around Halic, Galicia and Slovakia. Later he became one of the leaders of the Redemptorists in this region.

In 1950, the communist government of the Czech Republic, suppressed all the religious communities, and began persecuting Christians. Father Metod Dominik was also arrested and imprisoned.

During his time in prison, Father Metod Dominik was mistreated and even tortured physically and psychologically; so his health deteriorated. On his deathbed he

---

[4] *Butler's Lives of the Saints, New Full Edition*, [Revised by Kathleen Jones], June, Collegeville, Minnesota: The Liturgical Press, 1997, p. 169.

forgave all those who had persecuted him, and continuously prayed for them. He died on March 23, 1959.

St. Germaine Cousin of Pibrac

Germaine was born in 1579 in a small village in France called Pibrac. Germaine was born with a deformed and paralyzed right hand. To make matters worse, her mother died while Germaine was still very young.

After the death of her mother, her father married another woman. But this woman had no love at all for Germaine; she treated Germaine with cruelty. The young girl had to bear insults and all kinds of abuses from her stepmother.

Her father never said or did anything to protect her from being abused by her step-mother. He didn't seem to care at all. The child had no recourse.

Her stepmother always gave her very little food; so poor Germaine learned to crawl to the dog's dish so as to satisfy her hunger with the dog's food. There was a time when her stepmother left her in the drain for almost three days; and another time she intentionally poured boiling water on Germaine's legs.

As a result of this mistreatment from her stepmother, Germaine became weak and sickly. She had a disease called scrofula, a kind of tuberculosis. This caused ugly swellings and sores around her neck. Because of her weak body, she was always sickly. But her afflictions did not win sympathy from her father or stepmother.

Germaine was also tortured by her stepbrothers and stepsisters. They had learned from their mother how to despise and mistreat Germaine. They would beat her up, put ashes in her food, and make her clothes dirty. They were encouraged by their mother.

The stepmother did not want Germaine near her healthy children, so Germaine was forced to sleep in the stable with the sheep. She had no mattress, and during the cold winter nights, she slept as close to the sheep as possible to get some warmth from them. She was not allowed to eat with the family—alone in the stable, she ate the scraps of food that remained from the family's table.

When Germaine was about six years old, she was given the responsibility of taking care of the sheep. She never had the opportunity of going to school, but rather spent her days in the fields with the flock. However, in this loneliness she discovered God; as she tended the sheep, she talked to Him through her simple prayers. She made her own rosary, and loved the Blessed Virgin Mary very much.

Germaine would pray, "Dear God, I do not have anything to eat or drink; please don't let me be too hungry or thirsty. Help me to please my dear mother at home; and help me to please You, my dear God."

She had a great love for the Holy Eucharist and the Mass. Every day she fixed her shepherd staff in the ground, and make the sheep stand around it. Then she would ask Our Lord to take care of the sheep while she was at Mass. After Mass, she would come back and find her flock in the same place she had left them, without any sheep wandering away. The sheep were never attacked by wolves, although there were many in that place.

Germaine was generous, despite her poverty. She shared her scraps of food with other beggars. She often collected the children of the village to teach them about the love of Jesus and Mary.

In the Lives of the Saints, we read, "The adults of the village tended at first to accept her family's estimate of her as useless and diseased and to treat her with contempt and ridicule."[5] But gradually, when people saw how Germaine behaved, they realized that she was a holy girl.

Her stepmother was furious to hear people calling Germaine a saint, so she looked for opportunities to catch her doing something wrong. She wanted to discredit her stepchild in public.

One cold winter day, the stepmother caught Germaine carrying something in her apron, and immediately she thought she had stolen bread to feed her friends the beggars. She began to beat the girl, demanding that Germaine open her apron to show what she was carrying. When Germaine unfolded her apron, it was full of beautiful flowers that no one expected to see in wintertime.

Germaine picked one beautiful flower and gave it to her stepmother saying, "Please, my dear Mom, accept this flower; God sends this flower to you as a sign of His forgiveness to you. My dear Mom, I will always forgive you, and I will always love you."

It is amazing to see a young girl's heart so full of forgiveness for one who mistreated and tortured her.

People continued to talk about Germaine's holiness, so that her father and stepmother finally began to treat her better. They even asked her to sleep in the house. But Germaine turned down their invitation, and asked them to allow her to continue to sleep in the stable with the sheep, where she had slept for almost 17 years.

A few mornings later, she was found dead in the stable. She was only 22 years old, but her suffering had come to an end.

---

[5] *Butler's Lives of the Saints, New Full Edition*, [Revised by Kathleen Jones], June, Collegeville, Minnesota: The Liturgical Press, 1997, p. 115-116.

St. Agostina Pietrantoni

Saint Agostina was born in Italy on March 27, 1864. At the age of 22, she joined the Sisters of Charity. She was sent to work as a nurse in the hospital of Santo Spiritu (Holy Spirit Hospital) in Rome.

Agostina showed complete dedication and an extraordinary concern for the sick. She worked mainly among the critically ill and those with contagious diseases. Later she was asked to work in the tuberculosis ward.

One day while she was working, a man attacked her and stabbed her to death. But as she was dying, Agostina forgave her murderer, and prayed for his conversion.

Blessed Miguel Pro

Miguel was born in Mexico on January 13, 1891. In 1911, he joined the Jesuits, and began studying for the priesthood. When the religious persecution started in Mexico, Miguel and his fellow seminarians fled to the United States of America.

In 1915, he was sent to Spain to continue his priestly formation, which he completed in 1924. In 1926, he went to Belgium for his ordination.

He went back to Mexico that same year, despite the continual religious persecution. The churches had been closed and priests had gone into hiding. Father Miguel had to carry out his priestly ministry secretly.

Unfortunately, he was betrayed to the police, caught, and sentenced to death. Before he was executed, Father Miguel forgave his executioners and prayed for them.

St. Joseph Mukasa Balikuddembe

Mukasa was born around 1860 in Uganda. In 1874, he became a page for King Muteesa I. Mukasa was good at sports. Because of his intelligence, the Kabaka (king) gave him a number of important responsibilities.

In 1879, the Missionaries of Africa brought the Catholic Faith to Uganda; and Mukasa became a catechumen the following year. On April 30, 1882, Mukasa was baptized and given the name Joseph.

When the missionaries were temporarily chased out of the country, Mukasa became the leader and teacher of the Catholic community. He helped his fellow pages to grow in the Faith, and to start living a moral life in line with their Christian faith.

But in 1885, Kabaka Mwanga, who had succeeded Kabaka Muteesa I, started persecuting Christians. As a result, Mukasa was summoned and condemned to death.

"He was seized on a pretext and beheaded on November 15, 1885."[6] Before he died he forgave the king and prayed for his conversion. He was the first Ugandan Catholic to die for the Faith.

Blessed Josep Samso i Elias

Josep was born in Spain on January 17, 1887. During his priestly formation he was known to be a person of exemplary behavior, and a dedicated student. In 1909, Bishop Juan Jose Laguarda of Barcelona appointed him as his private secretary while he was yet a seminarian.

On March 12, 1910, Samso was ordained a priest. He served in several parishes and was known for his

---

[6] *Butler's Lives of the Saints, New Full Edition*, [Revised by Kathleen Jones], June, Collegeville, Minnesota: The Liturgical Press, 1997, p. 23.

dedication to the priestly ministry. He devoted himself to catechesis—teaching the catechism and guiding catechists.

In October, 1934, a group of armed men entered the Church of St. Mary, where Samso was pastor. They set the altar on fire and destroyed many other things. But Father Samso forgave them. He even refused the demands of the government authorities to reveal their identities.

A few months later, however, the Spanish civil war began in which the Catholic church was persecuted. In 1936, Father Samso was arrested and imprisoned because he was a priest.

He was condemned to death. Before he was killed, he asked to be untied so he could embrace his executioners. He hugged them and said, "I have forgiven you as Jesus forgave those who nailed Him on the Cross."

He died, forgiving and praying for his executioners, on September 1, 1936.

Blessed Margaret of Castello

Margaret was born toward the end of the thirteenth century in Italy, to noble parents who wanted a son. Her parents were horrified to find that not only was she a girl, but a blind, crippled and hunchbacked dwarf. The parents saw their daughter as a disgrace and a curse to their family. As a result, they decided to hide her in a secluded room so that nobody would ever know that she existed.

When she was six years old, however, she innocently came out of the room and made her presence known to guests who had come to visit her noble family. Her father was furious when he learned that his guests had seen her.

As a result, her father built a small room attached to the church, and he walled Margaret inside this room. It was tiny, with no door and only a small window. Her food and other necessities were passed in to her through this window. She could not come out because the window was too small—she was practically imprisoned.

The parish priest became a friend to Margaret, and talked to her every day through the little window. He helped her to learn more about her Faith and other things.

Later her parents took her to a shrine in Citta di Castello, where many sick people were being cured, to pray for her healing. But when she was not healed, her parents abandoned their blind, crippled daughter there. Fortunately, some good people came and took care of her.

She became a Dominican tertiary. We read,

> *From then on she lived a life wholly dedicated to God. She undertook the care and education of the local children, teaching them the psalms, which she had learned by heart, and trying to instill in them something of her own devotion to the Holy Child Jesus. She also visited the sick and those in prison. A number of miracles were attributed to her, including curing another tertiary of an affliction of the eyes, and it was said she experienced ecstasies and levitation while at prayer.* [7]

Despite the fact that her parents had abused, mistreated and abandoned her, Margaret was never bitter against her parents. She forgave them, prayed for them, and continued to love them dearly.

---

[7] *Butler's Lives of the Saints, New Full Edition*, [Revised by Kathleen Jones], April, Collegeville, Minnesota: The Liturgical Press, 1997, p. 95.

St. Wenceslaus

Wenceslaus was born around the year 902 in Bohemia (now the Czech Republic). His father was the Duke of Bohemia. His grandmother, Saint Ludmilla, made sure that Wenceslaus received a good Catholic education.

When his father was murdered, Wenceslaus became the new leader of Bohemia. He was known as "a good king." He loved his people and he loved the Catholic Faith. He was known for his virtues, and worked diligently to spread Christianity in his kingdom.

However, the anti-Christian party in his kingdom always opposed him and sought a way to kill him. His brother Boleslas also joined this anti-Christian party because he wanted to become the king of Bohemia.

In the lives of the Saints we read,

> *In September, 929,... Boleslas invited Wenceslaus to go to Stara Boleslav to celebrate the feast of Saints Cosmas and Damian... and the dedication of the church there. Next morning, on his way to Matins, he met Boleslas and thanked him for his hospitality. In response, Boleslas struck him and while the brothers struggled, friends of Boleslas ran up and killed Wenceslaus. As he fell at the chapel door, he murmured, 'Brother, may God forgive you.'* [8]

Wenceslaus sets us a great example of forgiving his brother and asking God's mercy for his soul.

---

[8] *Butler's Lives of the Saints, New Full Edition*, [Revised by Kathleen Jones], September, Collegeville, Minnesota: The Liturgical Press, 1997, p. 257.

Blessed Isidore Bakanja

Bakanja was born around 1887 in the Democratic Republic of Congo, which was at that time ruled by Belgium. At the age of 18, he converted to the Catholic faith, and was baptized on May 6, 1906.

Soon afterward, he became a catechist as he continued to work on the Belgian rubber plantation. He was a devout Christian and had a great devotion to the Blessed Virgin Mary. As a good and pious Catholic, he shared his Faith with his fellow workers on the plantation.

His Belgian employers were not happy to see him spreading the Faith. Christianity was seen as a threat to the power of the Belgian colonizers. These colonizers knew that they might not be able to exploit the black workers if these workers became Catholics. The Church was known to stand up for the rights of all those who were being oppressed.

Bakanja was ordered by his employers to stop catechizing. But Bakanja refused.

As a result, he was brutally beaten for teaching the Catholic Faith. The beating was so vicious that there was no hope of survival. But before he died, he forgave his attackers and promised to continue praying for them when he entered Heaven.

Blessed Margaret Pole

Margaret was born in England on August 14, 1473. She was the niece of Kings Edward IV and Richard III of England.

In 1491, Margaret married Sir Richard Pole, a great friend of the royal family. God blessed their marriage with five children. Some years later her husband died, and she was left to care for the children.

When King Henry VIII came to power, he respected Margaret very much. He considered her the holiest woman in England. But when he decided to divorce his wife and marry another woman, Margaret opposed him. She told the king that what he was doing was not right, because the sacrament of Matrimony is indissoluble.

The king was not happy to see Margaret opposing him, so he persecuted her and her family. Margaret was arrested and imprisoned. She was brutally mistreated, and even tortured.

On May 28, 1541, she was beheaded. Before she died, she forgave the king and all those who participated in her execution and prayed for all of them.

Blessed Titus Brandsma

Titus was born in the Netherlands on February 23, 1881. On September 17, 1898, he joined the Carmelites, and was ordained a priest in 1905.

After his ordination, he went to Rome for further studies, and earned a doctorate in philosophy in 1909. He later served as Rector Magnificus of the Catholic University of Nijmegen in the Netherlands.

During the second World War, he strongly opposed the Nazi ideology which he considered to be evil because it aimed at persecuting the Jews. He was committed to stopping the spread of Nazism.

He was arrested and put into a concentration camp. On July 26, 1942, he was killed by lethal injection. Like Jesus, Titus forgave his enemies before he died, giving a good example of forgiveness.

St. Antoninus

Saint Antoninus was born in Italy on March 1, 1489. From an early age he was considered intelligent, hardworking and holy.

At the age of 16, he entered the Dominican Order, and was a good example to all in the way he lived his religious life.

After some years he became the Archbishop of Florence. He was called the father of the poor because he never refused to help anyone who was in need.

He had a great love toward those who hated him. One of his enemies, a man called Ciardi, tried to assassinate him with a sword. Antoninus narrowly escaped when the sword pierced the chair where he was seated.

Antoninus forgave Ciardi and prayed for his conversion. The man completely repented, and became a religious of the Order of St. Francis.

Blessed Lucio Martinez Mancebo and Companions

In the 1930s, the Catholic Church faced persecution in Spain. On July 27, 1936, Father Lucio Martinez and his fellow Dominicans were arrested and imprisoned for the crime of being Catholic.

On July 29, 1936, Father Lucio, Father Felicisimo Diez Gonzalez and their companions were put on a truck and taken to the execution site. Unafraid to die for their Catholic Faith, they went singing.

In a spirit of true charity, Father Gonzalez gave a fountain pen as a gift to their executioners. When they reached the site, each priest forgave the firing squad. A few minutes later, the eight priests were gunned down.

St. Oliver Plunkett

Oliver was born in Ireland on November 1, 1629. In 1647 he went to Rome to study for the priesthood. When he completed his studies, he was ordained a priest on January 1, 1654.

The Irish bishops asked him to act as their representative in Rome. During this time, the English were persecuting Catholics in Ireland, so for many years he could not go back to his native country. He remained in Rome teaching theology in a university.

However, on July 9, 1669, he was appointed Archbishop of Armagh and Primate of all Ireland. He was officially consecrated on November 30. The following March, he finally went back to Ireland to take up his position as Archbishop and Primate.

When he arrived in his homeland, he immediately made efforts to rebuild the Catholic Church which was being persecuted. He set up new schools and frequently visited his flock to encourage them to be strong in their Faith. In his first four years as Archbishop, he administered the sacrament of Confirmation to more than 40,000 people.

The persecution of the Catholic Church in Ireland by the British intensified, but Archbishop Plunkett refused to abandon his people.

In 1679, he was arrested and put in prison, where he was brutally tortured. Finally on July 1, 1681, he was convicted of spreading the Catholic faith, and sentenced to death. At the scaffold, Archbishop Plunkett was asked whether he had anything to say about the sentence.

He stood up and said, "I accept the death penalty, but I also ask you to accept the forgiveness I am giving you now—know that I have forgiven you and I will continue to pray for you."

After saying those words, he was hanged and his body was cut into pieces.

St. Elizabeth of Portugal

Elizabeth was a Spanish Princess, born in 1271 in Spain. She was the daughter of Pedro III, king of Aragon. She grew up as a strictly religious person. She said the full Divine Office daily, always fasted and did a lot of penance.

At the age of 12, she married King Denis of Portugal. Elizabeth was a beautiful, charming and lovable wife, but above all she was a committed Catholic and always attended Mass. Unfortunately, her husband was not interested in religion, and was unfaithful to her. He committed the sin of adultery and fathered children outside marriage.

Elizabeth endured all this with patience and love. She continued to love and respect her husband, and prayed for him that he might start living a holy life.

She refused to become bitter and resentful toward her husband, but rather continually forgave him. Gradually the king was moved by her love and patience. He realized that he was living a sinful life, and hurting his wife. In the end he apologized to Elizabeth, and began living as a true Catholic.

When the king became sick, Elizabeth never left his side. She was there to take care of him until he died.

Nowadays when one finds out that his or her spouse is unfaithful, they often ask for a divorce or separation, with no forgiveness. Elizabeth forgave the unfaithfulness of her husband, and through that forgiveness and prayer, she helped her husband to become a better person.

St. Eustace White

Eustace was born around 1560 in England. His parents hated the Catholic Faith; so when Eustace became a Catholic, his father cursed him. Eventually, Eustace went to Rome to study for the priesthood, and after completing his studies, was ordained.

In November 1588, he came back to England to preach the gospel. But during this time Catholics were being persecuted; there was ill feeling toward Catholics all over England.

Eustace did his best to preach without fear. However, he was arrested for spreading the Catholic Faith in England. While in prison he was greatly tortured. He was later condemned to death. While he was still alive, his executioner started cutting off parts of his body so that he might die a slow and painful death. As his executioner was butchering him, Eustace forgave him and prayed for his conversion. He asked the Lord to bless him so that he might know the Truth and live according to that Truth.

St. Brice

Brice was born about the year 370 in France. He lost his parents when he was very young and was brought up by Saint Martin of Tours.

As a youth and young adult, he was problematic and difficult, and guilty of many crimes. He was disrespectful and insulting to Saint Martin, treating him with insolence and contempt. Saint Martin was Bishop of Tours and one of his clerics was Brice. Brice was wild, wicked, proud and ungrateful, abusing his guardian and referring to him as a foolish old man.

It was said that Brice always "…set himself up as a model because he had been brought up at Marmoutier—unlike

Martin, who, he pointed out contemptuously, had been brought up in the army camps and was becoming superstitious and foolish in his old age."[9]

One day, "Brice went round saying Martin was mad. When Martin asked him to justify his words, he denied that he had spoken them, to which Martin replied that he had heard them, adding, 'But I have prayed for you, and you shall be bishop of Tours.'"[10]

Some people asked Martin to dismiss Brice, but Martin always replied, "If Christ could tolerate Judas, surely I can put up with Brice."[11]

After some years, Brice came to his senses and realized that his behavior and way of treating Martin was wrong and sinful. He repented and went to Martin to ask for forgiveness. Martin readily forgave him. With this forgiveness, Brice became a good person; and when Saint Martin died, Brice succeeded him as Bishop of Tours.

St. Claudine Thevenet

Claudine was born in Lyon, France, on March 30, 1774. The Catholic Faith was firmly established in her family—hence she grew up a committed Christian. When she was about nine years old, her parents entrusted her to the Benedictine nuns of St. Peter's Abbey, in Place des Terreaux, where she received a solid spiritual and intellectual formation.

In 1789, when the French Revolution broke out, Claudine hastily returned to her family in Lyon. In 1793,

---

[9] *Butler's Lives of the Saints, New Full Edition,* [Revised by Kathleen Jones], November, Collegeville, Minnesota: The Liturgical Press, 1997, p. 102.

[10] *Ibid.*, p. 102.

[11] *Ibid.*, p. 102.

she experienced the tragic hours of the siege of Lyon by the government army.

Her two brothers were arrested and sentenced to death as enemies of the government. She was horrified to see them being taken to the execution site, and followed them closely, crying.

When the boys saw her, they shouted, "Forgive, as we also forgive!"

She responded, "My God, forgive these murderers, they do not know what they are doing."

That forgiveness brought peace in her life, as she helped her parents overcome the grief of losing two sons.

Blessed Peter of Castelnau

Peter was born in France in the twelfth century. Around 1202, he became a Cistercian monk. He was known as an intelligent and devout Catholic. In 1203, Pope Innocent III gave him the task of bringing the Albigensian heretics back to the Church.

Count Raymond VI of Toulouse, who for political reasons was on the side of the heretic Albigensians, continued to oppose moves against the heretics. It is believed that he ordered Peter's assassination. This was carried out on January 15, 1208, at Saint-Gilles on the Rhone, when he was run through with a lance.[12]

Peter's dying words were, "May God forgive thee, brother, as I fully forgave thee. I pray that we meet again in the Heavenly Kingdom."

---

[12] *Butler's Lives of the Saints, New Full Edition*, [Revised by Kathleen Jones], January, Collegeville, Minnesota: The Liturgical Press, 1997, p. 105.

St. John Grove

In the seventeenth century, Catholics were persecuted in England, and priests ministered to them at the risk of their lives. John Grove was a layman who owned a large house in London which he used as a secret home for Jesuit priests. He also attended to their daily needs.

However, on September 28, 1678, John Grove, Father William Ireland, Father John Fenwick and others were arrested and put in prison. They were tortured and then condemned to death for being Catholics.

We read, "Ireland and Grove were hanged, drawn and quartered at Tyburn on January 24, 1679."[13] Before dying, Grove said, "We are innocent, but we pray that God may forgive all those who have caused this."

---

[13] *Butler's Lives of the Saints, New Full Edition*, [Revised by Kathleen Jones], January, Collegeville, Minnesota: The Liturgical Press, 1997, p. 165.

PART II

Forgiveness in the New Testament

Matthew 5: 36-42 – Teaching About Retaliation............. 37
Matthew 5: 43-48 – Love Your Enemies.................... 38
Matthew 6: 12 -15 – The Lord's Prayer 39
Matthew 18: 21-35 – The Parable of the Unforgiving Servant... 40
Romans 12:14-21 – Mutual Love.......................... 45

PART II

Forgiveness in the New Testament

Forgiveness is not man's creation, it is God's creation. God has always wanted His people to live in that spirit of forgiving one another. In the New Testament, we have many passages that emphasize this idea, including these:

Matthew 5:36-42 – Teaching About Retaliation

> 36 Do not swear by your head, for you cannot make a single hair white or black. 37 Let your 'Yes' mean 'Yes,' and your 'No' mean 'No.' Anything more is from the evil one.
> 38 You have heard that it was said, 'An eye for an eye and a tooth for a tooth.' 39 But I say to you, offer no resistance to one who is evil. When someone strikes you on (your) right cheek, turn the other one to him as well. 40 If anyone wants to go to law with you over your tunic, hand him your cloak as well. 41 Should anyone press you into service for one mile, go with him for two miles. 42 Give to the one who asks of you, and do not turn your back on one who wants to borrow.

In these verses Jesus teaches us how we should respond to those who sin against us. The essence of His Teaching in this regard is that we should love them, and never commit the sin of revenge. Jesus gives us examples:

> 38 "You have heard that it was said, 'An eye for an eye and a tooth for a tooth.' 39 But I say to you, offer no resistance to one who is evil. When someone strikes you on (your) right cheek, turn the other one to him as well."

By turning the other cheek, we overcome evil with good, as Saint Paul says in Romans 12:21:

> 21 Do not be conquered by evil but conquer evil with good.

Jesus is the best example for us—He was hurt and humiliated in so many ways. He had the ability to retaliate, but He chose not to do so. He chose to overcome evil with good. Every time we sin, we are slapping Our Lord in the Face, but He does not retaliate. Instead He turns the other Cheek and continues to do good for us, giving us the sun, rain, life, and everything we have.

Matthew 5:43-48 – Love Your Enemies

> 43 "You have heard that it was said, 'You shall love your neighbor and hate your enemy.' 44 But I say to you, love your enemies, and pray for those who persecute you, 45 that you may be children of your Heavenly Father, for He makes His sun rise on the bad and the good, and causes rain to fall on the just and the unjust. 46 For if you love those who love you, what recompense will you have? Do not the tax collectors do the same? 47 And if you greet your brothers only, what is unusual about that? Do not the pagans do the same? 48 So be perfect, just as your Heavenly Father is perfect."

By asking us to love our enemies, Jesus shows that He expects us to forgive those who have sinned against us:

> 43 "You have heard that it was said, 'You shall love your neighbor and hate your enemy.' 44 But I say to you, love your enemies, and pray for those who persecute you, 45 that you may be children of your Heavenly Father, for He makes

His sun rise on the bad and the good, and causes rain to fall on the just and the unjust."

By loving our enemies, we qualify as true children of God. Likewise if we refuse to love, we disqualify ourselves as His true children.

We should not only forgive by words, but also by our actions, for example, "Pray for those who persecute you." Prayer helps us to move away from the contemplation of revenge to thoughts of forgiving and loving our enemies.

As we pray for our enemies, God speaks to us, and we begin to see our enemies as God sees them. God loves them too, and if we can learn to see them as God sees them, then our love for them will grow. God asks us to do this because He Himself loves His enemies:

45 ... for He makes His sun rise on the bad and the good, and causes rain to fall on the just and the unjust.

Because of our sins, we have all been enemies of God, but God went the extra mile to show His love for us. He sent His Son to die for us, His enemies, so that we might be saved.

Hence, God does not only bless His Friends, but He also loves and blesses His enemies—and He asks us to do the same. By loving our enemies, we become witnesses for God's love.

Matthew 6:12-15 – The Lord's Prayer

12 and forgive us our debts, as we forgive our debtors;
13 and do not subject us to the final test, but deliver us from the evil one.
14 If you forgive others their transgressions, your Heavenly Father will forgive you. 15 But if you do not forgive others, neither will your Father forgive your transgressions.

Because of the importance of forgiving one another, when Jesus was teaching His disciples how to pray, He included the issue of forgiveness in the prayer He taught them.

In this prayer it is clear that since we need forgiveness from our God, we should also be ready to offer that same forgiveness to our neighbors:

> 12 and forgive us our debts, as we forgive our debtors;

By saying this phrase we either condemn ourselves or absolve ourselves. If we fail to forgive others, it's as if we are telling God not to forgive our sins. This is terrible, because we sin always, and therefore, we always need God's forgiveness to live. We must forgive others so as to win God's favor, and make our prayers meaningful.

> 14 If you forgive others their transgressions, your Heavenly Father will forgive you. 15 But if you do not forgive others, neither will your Father forgive your transgressions.

To ask God for forgiveness when we ourselves do not offer it to our neighbors, is an insult to Almighty God.

Matthew 18:21-35 – The Parable of the Unforgiving Servant

> 21 Then Peter approaching asked him, "Lord, if my brother sins against me, how often must I forgive him? As many as seven times?" 22 Jesus answered, "I say to you, not seven times but seventy-seven times. 23 That is why the Kingdom of Heaven may be likened to a king who decided to settle accounts with his servants. 24 When he began the accounting, a debtor was brought before him who owed him a huge amount. 25 Since he had no way of paying it back, his master ordered him to be sold, along with his wife, his children, and all his property, in payment of the debt. 26 At that, the servant fell down, did him homage, and said, 'Be patient with me, and I will pay you back in full.' 27 Moved with compassion the master of that servant let him go and forgave him the loan. 28 When that servant had left, he found one of his fellow servants who owed him a much smaller amount. He seized him and started to choke him,

demanding, 'Pay back what you owe.' ²⁹ Falling to his knees, his fellow servant begged him, 'Be patient with me, and I will pay you back.' ³⁰ But he refused. Instead, he had him put in prison until he paid back the debt. ³¹ Now when his fellow servants saw what had happened, they were deeply disturbed, and went to their master and reported the whole affair. ³² His master summoned him and said to him, 'You wicked servant! I forgave you your entire debt because you begged me to. ³³ Should you not have had pity on your fellow servant, as I had pity on you?' ³⁴ Then in anger his master handed him over to the torturers until he should pay back the whole debt. ³⁵ So will My Heavenly Father do to you, unless each of you forgives his brother from his heart."

Here in the Gospel of Saint Matthew, we find a number of Jesus' sayings on how His Disciples are supposed to live and treat one another to build a community. The last part of chapter 18 deals with forgiveness, because without it we cannot have a community. A community is built on forgiveness, because we are human beings and not angels. We continually injure one another in different ways; these injuries can easily break up the community. Hence we must forgive one another continually so as to sustain the community.

After listening to Jesus speak about the importance of forgiving one another, Peter wanted to know if there is any limit on this issue of forgiveness:

²¹ Then Peter approaching asked him, "Lord, if my brother sins against me, how often must I forgive him? As many as seven times?"

By suggesting the limit for forgiveness to be seven times, Peter was being more generous than the Jewish laws of that time. During that time the Jewish rabbis taught that it was enough to forgive someone three times.

Peter may have thought that by suggesting to forgive seven times, Jesus would be pleased with him. Seven times was more than the law required, and the number seven indicates perfection, so by forgiving seven times, one would achieve a "perfect forgiveness."

However, Jesus told Peter that forgiving seven times may seem like a lot, but it is not enough.

> 22 Jesus answered, "I say to you, not seven times but seventy-seven times."

In other words, we are called to forgive without limit, without counting. That is the way God deals with us—God is always ready to forgive us without counting how many times we have offended Him. He wants to see that same attitude in us. God wants us to forgive others countless times.

Lack of forgiveness has contributed a great deal to the misery in this world. If everyone grew in the habit of forgiving others without limit, we could eliminate a lot of suffering caused by disputes, quarrels, disagreements, misunderstandings, insults, offenses and provocations.

In Matthew 18, Jesus teaches us that Christians need to forgive one another, or they will bring more suffering to themselves because of their unforgiveness. Jesus starts the parable by saying:

> 23 That is why the kingdom of heaven may be likened to a king who decided to settle accounts with his servants. 24When he began the accounting, a debtor was brought before him who owed him a huge amount.

In this parable the king represents God, and the servant represents any Christian who needs forgiveness from God because of his or her sins. In verse 24, the "huge amount" owed, was equal to 10,000 talents.

One talent was equal to 6,000 denarii—this means that 10,000 talents was equal to 60,000,000 denarii. A year's wage for a servant was about 600 denarii. This means that in order to pay a debt of 60,000,000 denarii, one would have to work for 100,000 years. The amount that the servant owed to his master was impossible to pay—there was no way he was going to work for 100,000 years to pay this debt.

The servant's enormous debt represents our massive debt to God because of the sins we commit every single day—in our actions, thoughts, and words.

The king in the parable initially sets out to punish this servant who owed him a lot of money, as we see here:

> 25 Since he had no way of paying it back, his master ordered him to be sold, along with his wife, his children, and all his property, in payment of the debt.

But the servant begs for more time to pay the debt:

> 26 At that, the servant fell down, did him homage, and said, 'Be patient with me, and I will pay you back in full.'

Considering the size of the amount owed, the servant's plea for more time, and his promise to pay all the debt, was a lie. No one can work for 100,000 years. He was promising the impossible. What the servant really needed from the king was not more time, but mercy and forgiveness.

Although the servant did not ask for mercy, the king responded with it:

> 27 Moved with compassion the master of that servant let him go and forgave him the loan.

The servant received more than he asked for—all his debt was canceled without any condition on it, and he was set free.

It is interesting to see how this servant responded to the forgiveness he had received. We are not even told whether he thanked the king. Instead we are told that:

> 28 When that servant had left, he found one of his fellow servants who owed him a much smaller amount. He seized him and started to choke him, demanding, 'Pay back what you owe.'

This shows that the forgiven servant had not appreciated the mercy shown him. His fellow servant owed him just one hundred denarii, a very small amount compared to the amount of 60,000,000 denarii which he had owed to his king.

It would take 100,000 years to pay 60,000,000 denarii, whereas it would take only two months to pay back 100 denarii.

His fellow servant pleaded for more time:

> ²⁹ Falling to his knees, his fellow servant begged him, 'Be patient with me, and I will pay you back.'

This is exactly the same plea the forgiven servant made to the king. But the forgiven servant's debt had been too much; he had no way of paying it. His fellow servant had the possibility of paying the debt of 100 denarii if given time.

The wicked servant, however, had no intention of showing mercy to his companion:

> ³⁰ But he refused. Instead, he had him put in prison until he paid back the debt.

This parable shows how human beings sometimes operate—they are eager and ready to receive forgiveness from God, but are not always ready to give that same forgiveness to their neighbors. People are too often prone to condemn, hold grudges and seek revenge.

When the forgiven servant refused to forgive his fellow servant who owed him a small amount, the other servants were shocked by this lack of forgiveness. They took action against the forgiven servant:

> ³¹ Now when his fellow servants saw what had happened, they were deeply disturbed, and went to their master and reported the whole affair. ³² His master summoned him and said to him, 'You wicked servant! I forgave you your entire debt because you begged me to. ³³ Should you not have had pity on your fellow servant, as I had pity on you?' ³⁴ Then in anger his master handed him over to the torturers until he should pay back the whole debt.

Hence, the forgiven servant, who had at first escaped suffering, ends up suffering because of his unforgiveness. If we refuse to forgive others, we show that we have not really understood the value of the forgiveness given to us by our God, and we bring suffering to ourselves.

Jesus brings home the point of the entire parable when He says:

> 35 "So will My Heavenly Father do to you, unless each of you forgives his brother from his heart."

Romans 12:14-21 – Mutual Love

> 14 Bless those who persecute (you), bless and do not curse them. 15 Rejoice with those who rejoice, weep with those who weep. 16 Have the same regard for one another; do not be haughty but associate with the lowly; do not be wise in your own estimation. 17 Do not repay anyone evil for evil; be concerned for what is noble in the sight of all. 18 If possible, on your part, live at peace with all. 19 Beloved, do not look for revenge but leave room for the wrath; for it is written, "Vengeance is mine, I will repay, says the Lord." 20 Rather, "if your enemy is hungry, feed him; if he is thirsty, give him something to drink; for by so doing you will heap burning coals upon his head." 21 Do not be conquered by evil but conquer evil with good.

In these verses, Saint Paul lays out what a Christian should do to those who sin against him:

> 14 Bless those who persecute (you), bless and do not curse them.

This is a command which we have to fulfill as Christians. Paul doesn't write, "you may bless them," he says rather "Bless them." In other words, instead of wishing the worst for our enemies, we are called upon to pray for their well-being and sincerely desire their happiness.

However, "bless them" does not only mean to pray for them, but also entails doing good for them in our actions, even though we may not like them.

From a human point of view, it seems impossible to bless our enemies, but with God nothing is impossible. We need to ask Our Lord to give us the grace to bless our enemies instead of cursing them.

> [17] Do not repay anyone evil for evil…

Evil begets evil. A Christian should aim at overcoming evil with something good, so we are not allowed to seek revenge. Jesus gives us the best example, as Peter points out in 1 Peter 2:

> [23] When He was insulted, He returned no insult; when He suffered, He did not threaten; instead, He handed Himself over to the One who judges justly.

In these verses, Paul encourages us to live in harmony and peace, even with those who have sinned against us:

> [19] Beloved, do not look for revenge but leave room for the wrath; for it is written, "Vengeance is mine, I will repay, says the Lord." [20] Rather, "if your enemy is hungry, feed him; if he is thirsty, give him something to drink; for by so doing you will heap burning coals upon his head."

When we are treated maliciously, we are not to take revenge ourselves, but instead, we should let God do what He Wills. This means we should let God act on our behalf; we should get out of the way and let God do His part. But we are not only called to refrain from acts of revenge; we also must remove from our hearts all thoughts and desires of revenge.

Our good behavior toward our enemies will prove that we are not interested in revenge, and that we have left God to do the repayment. This is why Saint Paul says:

> [20] Rather, "if your enemy is hungry, feed him; if he is thirsty, give him something to drink; for by so doing you will heap burning coals upon his head."

These acts of charity demonstrate that we are at peace with leaving the retaliation to God. Loving our enemies is at the very core of our Christian faith – and it is one of the major proofs that we are true disciples of Christ, true Christians.

Showing love for our enemy is the most effective way to subdue him. The love we show to our enemy will do more to change his behavior than the sword of revenge. Our love will melt his heart and bring remorse and shame for his evil, much more effectively than the fire of our wrath.

Christ, again, is our example in this. We are all His enemies, *"for all have sinned"* (Rom. 3:23), but rather than hurling down the fire of wrath on us, Christ rains upon us His Love, by feeding us when we are hungry, giving us drink when we thirst, giving us the sun and the rain, and our entire being.

PART III

Reflections on Forgiving One Another

Forgiveness Promotes Life. 51
Forgiveness is More Important than Sacrifice 54
Forgiveness Brings Healing. 55
A Command to Forgive. 59
We Are All Sinners. 62
A Forgiveness That Restores Relationships. 63
A Forgiveness that Aims at the Conversion of Others 65
Some Of The Consequences Of Unforgiveness 66

PART III

Reflections on Forgiving One Another

Forgiveness Promotes Life

Whenever we offer forgiveness to our brothers and sisters, we promote life in them; when we refuse forgiveness to our brothers and sisters, we are in a way destroying the life in them. When we forgive, it's as if we are giving them the chance to continue living.

John 8:1-11 "A Woman Caught in Adultery"

This is a good example of how forgiveness can save a life or promote life. The woman who was caught in adultery was going to be stoned to death, but when Jesus offered her forgiveness, her life was spared. She became a better person and began to lead a holy life.

> 1 while Jesus went to the Mount of Olives. 2 But early in the morning He arrived again in the temple area, and all the people started coming to Him, and He sat down and taught them. 3 Then the scribes and the Pharisees brought a woman who had been caught in adultery and made her stand in the middle. 4 They said to Him, "Teacher, this

woman was caught in the very act of committing adultery. 5 Now in the law, Moses commanded us to stone such women. So what do you say?" 6 They said this to test Him, so that they could have some charge to bring against Him. Jesus bent down and began to write on the ground with His Finger. 7 But when they continued asking Him, He straightened up and said to them, "Let the one among you who is without sin be the first to throw a stone at her." 8 Again He bent down and wrote on the ground. 9 And in response, they went away one by one, beginning with the elders. So He was left alone with the woman before Him. 10 Then Jesus straightened up and said to her, "Woman, where are they? Has no one condemned you?" 11 She replied, "No one, sir." Then Jesus said, "Neither do I condemn you. Go, (and) from now on do not sin any more."

By forgiving this woman, Jesus gave her a chance to continue living; and this forgiveness changed her into a better person. The physical life of this woman was saved, but Jesus also renewed her spiritual life by forgiving her sins.

A Missed Opportunity to Save a Life

I remember serving as a supply priest in one of the parishes in Europe for two months. One Friday night at around 9 pm, a phone rang.

When I picked it up, a man said, "I would like to speak to the pastor, please."

I went to inform the pastor, but he told me that the man should call him later because he was having an important meeting.

"I will not be able to ring later," the caller responded, "But I am going to leave a message for the pastor with you if you do not mind."

The man told me his name, and then said, "Tell the pastor that I was only looking for forgiveness, but it seems that nobody is interested."

I waited for him to continue, but he put down the phone. I was confused. I couldn't make sense of the one sentence that he'd said, and I didn't have his telephone number to call him back. Later, I told the pastor what the man had said.

"What was his name?" he asked, and upon hearing it, "Aha, I know him. He is one of those people who were convicted of sexual abuse. He accepted the crime, and was sent to prison. Last year he was released from prison after serving his sentence. I'm sure he will ring again."

But the man never called again. In fact, the following day he was found dead. He left the same message for a number of people. He also wrote it down in detail, and left it on the table.

This man probably couldn't find anyone to tell him, "What you did was wrong, but I forgive you. I will accompany you in this journey of conversion you have begun."

I am sure some people were ready to forgive him, but they were not ready to associate with him or be near him. Some people probably were protecting themselves; they didn't want their names to be tainted. People may have thought that if they associated themselves with this man, others might think that they were guilty of similar sins. So in a way, they said, "We forgive you, but do not come near us—stay away."

Others only wanted to condemn him forever, symbolically stoning him to death like the people in the gospel who wanted to stone the adulterous woman. I think that the man didn't want to wait to be "stoned to death," so he went....

Maybe if this man had found someone who was ready to forgive him and accompany him on the long road of repentance, it would have saved his life. The adulterous woman in the gospel was blessed because Jesus was there to forgive her and to accompany her in the journey.

Jesus knew that His Name would be tainted if He associated Himself with this sinful woman—but that did not make Jesus prefer protecting His Name. Jesus would rather lose His reputation than lose this woman—instead of saving His Name, He preferred to save the woman. The forgiveness of Jesus renewed the physical and spiritual life in this woman.

Forgiveness renews our physical and spiritual life. For example, when we confess our sins in the Sacrament of Penance, we feel relieved and renewed. Hence, when we forgive others we offer them life. When we deny them forgiveness we deny them life.

Forgiveness is More Important than Sacrifice

Sacrifices offered with a heart full of resentment and hatred are not pleasing to God. That is why, at the beginning of Mass, we first seek reconciliation with God and with our neighbors, so that our sacrifice may be meaningful and pleasing to God.

In Matthew 5:23-24, Jesus says,

> [23] "Therefore, if you bring your gift to the altar, and there recall that your brother has anything against you, [24] leave your gift there at the altar, go first and be reconciled with your brother, and then come and offer your gift."

This passage clearly shows the importance of forgiveness, and shows how Jesus was serious about forgiveness. Jesus made it clear that if we want to bring our prayer, offering or sacrifice at the altar, we'd better first forgive one another.

In fact, if sacrifice was more important than forgiveness, Jesus could have said, "You want to bring your sacrifice at the altar, but you have not reconciled with your neighbor. It is all right for you first to bring your offering, and then go back and reconcile with your neighbor."

But Jesus did not say that; He said the opposite. In effect, He said, "If you have not reconciled with your neighbor, leave your offering there. I do not even want to look at it until you have reconciled with your neighbor. I want an offering or a prayer that is offered *in* love and *with* love. That is the offering that pleases Me. That is the offering that will bring blessings in your life."

This is why at the beginning of Mass, we ask for forgiveness, so that our prayer may be acceptable to God. If we do not ask for forgiveness first, all our prayers will be meaningless.

Forgiveness Brings Healing

A Woman With AIDS

In 2003, I went to the hospital to anoint a friend of mine who was suffering from cancer. Afterwards, I spent some time with him even though he could not talk.

As I was about to leave, a lady came to me and said, "Father, there is someone in the next room who wants to talk to a priest."

When I entered the next room, I almost fainted. A woman lay in the bed, her body covered with sores. I thought, *If she needs to be anointed, where am I going to touch?*

I greeted her, and there was a moment of silence. Then the patient said, "Father, my husband infected me with AIDS. He has already admitted it, and has repeatedly apologized to me, but I find it very hard to forgive him. I have even refused to let him come here to see me. I do not want to see him. But at the same time I know that I'm about to die, and I do not want to die with this hatred in my heart. Please, what can I do? I find it hard to forgive him."

At first I really didn't know what to say. But then I told her that I also struggle with forgiveness. It is not easy to forgive, especially a close friend or a relative.

"Continue asking God to give you the grace to forgive," I said. I asked her to say a rosary novena asking Our Mother Mary to intercede for her so that she might be able to forgive. I said that after the novena, she must tell her husband that she has forgiven him. "After telling your husband that you have forgiven him, then leave it to Our Lord to do the rest—He will complete the process of forgiveness which He has started in you."

She promised me that she would do what I had asked. But after looking at the terrible condition of her health, I felt certain that she wouldn't be able to finish the novena. Something told me that she would die in a few days.

My consolation was that she would die while praying for forgiveness, instead of dying while contemplating revenge or bitterness. Praying for forgiveness would take her closer to God, while bitterness would take her away from God.

Three weeks later, I came back to see my sick friend. Afterwards, I again went to the room of the lady with AIDS to see whether she was still there. To my surprise, when I entered the room she was still alive. There was a man with her, and they were both crying bitterly. I left, telling myself that I would come back another time.

The following day I went back to see her, and she greeted me with a big smile. I could see the joy and happiness in her eyes.

"I did what you told me," she said, "And yesterday I called my husband and told him that I forgave him. We talked and cried for hours, but I think we cried more than we talked. He also asked for forgiveness, and I accepted his request."

She continued, "And at the end of it all, I felt that my heart was light. I felt peace and joy. Despite being sick, I felt more life in me as if I was cured. But I think it is the joy I had in my heart that made me forget about my physical pains. Now I'm ready to die in peace, and with peace in my heart."

I asked her whether she had received the Sacrament of the Anointing of the Sick, and she said no. I gave her my telephone number, and told her that anytime that she felt ready to receive the sacrament, I would be willing to help her.

One Sunday evening as I was preparing to have my dinner, she called me and said, "Father, I know you may not believe it, but since the day I forgave my husband, my life has become better and better. The doctors told me that I should even stop taking the medicine, and I was discharged from the hospital!"

"Yesterday," she went on, "I went back to the hospital for a checkup and I was told that it seems I no longer have the AIDS virus! But they told me to come back after six months to do more tests."

Although I found it hard to believe that she was cured of the AIDS virus, I was very impressed by the improvement of her life so soon after she had decided to forgive. I had been so sure that she was going to die within a few days or weeks.

I went to see her and I was amazed. She was well again. I could see the scars of the wounds, but they were also fading away. She was full of life—you would never think that she was the one who had been dying a few days ago.

All this healing started on the day she forgave her husband. At first she thought that forgiveness would only bring peace of mind. She had no way of knowing that that same forgiveness would also bring about physical and spiritual renewal. The forgiveness opened up God's healing and blessings in her.

St. Maxellendis

Saint Maxellendis lived in the seventh century. She was born into a noble family. Her father was called Humolin, and her mother was Ameltrudis.

When she reached the age of marriage, her parents wanted her to marry a man called Harduin of Solesmes.

But Maxellendis told her parents that she wanted to become a nun. When Maxellendis saw that her parents were really determined to make her marry Harduin, she ran away from home and went into hiding.

Unfortunately, we read in the lives of the saints that,

> *Harduin and his friends discovered her hiding place, broke in, and carried her off. She managed to break loose and was running away when Harduin, furious now, struck her with his sword. The force of the blow killed her instantly, and Harduin himself went blind on the spot.* [14]

After her burial, a lot of miracles started happening at her tomb. Bishop Vindician of Cambrai organized a procession to translate the relics of Maxellendis to the church of St. Vaast at Caudry.

The blind Harduin asked to be led out to meet the procession. When he reached her coffin, he fell on his knees, acknowledging his crime and asking for forgiveness. Immediately his sight was restored. Forgiveness had brought healing into his life.

Blessed John Licci

He was born in Italy in 1400. We read that "his mother died giving him birth, and his father, whether because he was in a state of shock after his wife's death or because the family was too poor, provided no proper care for the child."[15]

It is said that one day a neighbor lady found baby John crying and alone at home, because his father had

---

[14] *Butler's Lives of the Saints, New Full Edition*, [Revised by Kathleen Jones], November, Collegeville, Minnesota: The Liturgical Press, 1997, p. 104.

[15] *Butler's Lives of the Saints, New Full Edition*, [Revised by Kathleen Jones], November, Collegeville, Minnesota: The Liturgical Press, 1997, p. 116.

gone to work. This lady took John into her home and fed him. Then she laid him on the bed next to her paralyzed husband, and instantly the man was cured.

From that day onward, John's life was full of miracles. Even when he later became a Dominican priest, Our Lord continued to use him in a miraculous way.

One day, John was attacked by bandits. One tried to stab the priest, but his hand withered and became paralyzed instantly. When the bandit realized what had happened, he fell down on his knees and asked John to forgive him. John made the sign of the cross on the bandit, and said, "I forgive you."

At that very moment, the man's hand was healed. Forgiveness had once more brought healing.

A Command to Forgive

Forgiving others is not something we may choose to do or not do—it is not an option. It is a command from our Lord and God, Jesus Christ, so we are obliged to fulfill this command. If I refuse to obey this precept, I am going against Jesus, and committing a sin.

> "Be on your guard! If your brother sins, rebuke him; and if he repents, forgive him. And if he wrongs you seven times in one day and returns to you seven times saying, 'I am sorry', you should forgive him." (Luke 17:3-4)

In the above passage from the Gospel of Luke, Jesus is not saying that you *may* forgive, Jesus is saying that you *should* forgive. It is a "must," not a "maybe."

Jesus said we must forgive—therefore forgiving becomes an act of obedience. Jesus wants us to have a good relationship with one another—and forgiveness can act as an oil to lubricate those difficult relationships. Forgiveness keeps these relationships from becoming dry and corroded by hate, retribution and anger. Hence, we should not harbor any form of unforgiveness in our hearts.

Saint Paul stresses this command of forgiving when he says:

> Put on then, as God's chosen ones, holy and beloved, heartfelt compassion, kindness, humility, gentleness, and patience, bearing with one another and forgiving one another, if one has a grievance against another; as the Lord has forgiven you, so must you also do. (Colossians 3:12-13)

Letting the offender "off the hook"

There are those who ignore this command, because they have been hurt so deeply. Some think that they are justified in refusing to forgive, as a way of punishing the offender. These people think that by forgiving the offender, they are letting the offender "off the hook."

Yes, forgiveness will free the offender from blame before the one he has offended, but it will not free him from blame before God. God requires the offender to repent.

The command is to forgive not only those who slightly injure us, but also those who gravely injure us. We are called to forgive all, irrespective of what they have done to us – and we are called to forgive always.

> "Then Peter approaching asked him, 'Lord, if my brother sins against me, how often must I forgive him? As many as seven times?' Jesus answered, 'I say to you, not seven times but seventy-seven times.'" (Matthew 18:21-22)

Saint Paul says to forgive every offense, in Colossians 3:12-13:

> [12] Put on then, as God's chosen ones, holy and beloved, heartfelt compassion, kindness, humility, gentleness, and patience, [13] bearing with one another and forgiving one another, if one has a grievance against another; as the Lord has forgiven you, so must you also do.

The Offender Did Not Ask for Forgiveness

There is also a tendency to ignore the command to forgive, with the excuse that the other party did not apologize or accept the wrong he has committed.

But even if the offender does not ask for forgiveness, or does not accept his mistake, we are supposed to forgive. We should always be ready to take forgiveness to the offender even before he asks.

Jesus Himself gave us forgiveness when we were still sinners. He did not wait for us to change. He gave us His forgiveness before we asked for it. Jesus doesn't ask us to do something He Himself wouldn't do; He asks us to follow His Example.

> "For Christ, while we were still helpless, yet died at the appointed time for the ungodly. Indeed, only with difficulty does one die for a just person, though perhaps for a good person one might even find courage to die. But God proves His Love for us in that while we were still sinners Christ died for us." (Romans 5:6-8)

On the Cross Jesus said,

> "Father, forgive them, they know not what they do."
> (Luke 23:34)

Jesus forgave those who crucified Him, even before they asked for forgiveness. Jesus did not wait for them to say, "We are sorry." He offered them forgiveness then and there while they were crucifying Him.

Hence, it is wrong to think, "Well, this person sinned against me, so let him or her take the initiative of seeking forgiveness." Was God not the Offended One? Yet did He not come from Heaven to seek and save the sinner? We too are called to take forgiveness to those who have sinned against us. There is no situation where the Lord does not expect us to forgive.

"I will Forgive when He Stops Hurting Me"

There are those who say that they will only forgive if the person stops hurting them. They question, "Must I forgive if a person continues to hurt me?" The answer is "Yes." While hanging on the Cross, Jesus forgave His enemies, though they continued to spit at Him and abuse Him. Read Luke 23:34-37:

> 34 [Then Jesus said, "Father, forgive them, they know not what they do."] They divided His Garments by casting lots. 35 The people stood by and watched; the rulers, meanwhile, sneered at Him and said, "He saved others, let Him save Himself if He is the Chosen One, the Messiah of God." 36 Even the soldiers jeered at Him. As they approached to offer Him wine 37 they called out, "If you are King of the Jews, save yourself."

We see that Jesus did not wait for them to stop abusing Him before He forgave. As followers of Christ, we are called to do the same.

We Are All Sinners

The universality of sin should make us more generous and forgiving toward our neighbors. We are all sinners, and we all need forgiveness. The Psalmist says:

> Out of the depths I call to You, Lord; Lord, hear my cry! May Your Ears be attentive to my cry for mercy. If You, Lord should mark our guilt, who would survive? But with You is forgiveness and so You are revered. (Psalm 130:1-4)

In other words, if the Lord were to cut off one part of our bodies every time we commit a sin, no one would live. But the forgiving Father keeps on forgiving us. Hence, we are alive because of God's mercy. This knowledge should compel us to show that same mercy to those who sin against us.

In the Mass we pray, "Do not consider what we truly deserve, but grant us Your Forgiveness."

We are not only asking the Lord to not punish us; we are asking Him to not even *consider* punishing us for our sins. We want Our Lord to only think about forgiving us. If we desire so much forgiveness from God, we should also be ready to give that same forgiveness to our brothers and sisters who sin against us.

In the eighth chapter of Saint John's Gospel, Jesus asked the people who wanted to stone the adulterous woman to first see whether they themselves had committed no sin. When these people examined their consciences, they found that they were as guilty as the woman. They walked away in shame, realizing that they themselves needed forgiveness for their sins, just like the woman caught in adultery.

A Forgiveness That Restores Relationships

There are a lot of people who say, "I forgive you, but do not come near me. I don't want to be in contact with you; I don't want to have anything to do with you. I will keep you at arm's length, but I have forgiven you."

This is not the kind of forgiveness that God expects us to offer to our brothers and sisters, however. God expects us to offer a forgiveness that makes an effort to restore a relationship which has been damaged.

God wants us to live in a community of love, not as selfish individuals. God wants us to help each other to Heaven. That is why when Jesus was going back to Heaven, He stressed that we should remain *one*. When our relationships with our brethren break down, it is our duty to make an effort to rebuild them.

When God gave us His Forgiveness, He did not say: "I have forgiven you, but I do not want to have any thing to do with you."

Instead He said, "I forgive you, and I will come and live among you so as to rebuild our relationship."

In the Biblical story of Gomer & Hosea, we see this type of forgiveness that aims at restoring a relationship. Gomer was the wife of the prophet Hosea, but she was unfaithful. In fact, she abandoned Hosea with their three children, and pursued a life of prostitution. In the end, her sinful companions completely rejected her, and plotted to sell her as a slave.

Hosea, however, forgave his wife, and bought her from those people who wanted to sell her into slavery.

> Again the Lord said to me: Give your love to a woman beloved of a paramour, an adulteress; Even as the Lord loves the people of Israel, though they turn to other gods and are fond of raisin cakes. So I bought her for fifteen pieces of silver and homer and a lethech of barley. Then I said to her: Many days you shall wait for me; you shall not play the harlot Or belong to any man; I in turn will wait for you. (Hosea 3:1-3)

Hosea not only forgave his wife, but took the initiative to restore their relationship. He didn't say to his wife: "I have forgiven you, but I do not want to have anything to do with you." Instead, Hosea welcomed his wife back into his life.

We see this same forgiveness in the parable of the prodigal son, in Luke 15:11-32. His father did not just forgive him and keep him at arm's length. He welcomed his son back into the community of love—he took steps to restore the relationship with his son.

> "While he was still a long way off, his father caught sight of him, and was filled with compassion. He ran to his son, and embraced him and kissed him." (Luke 15:20)

This embrace of the father, was a sign that he was interested in rebuilding the relationship. Even a feast is prepared so as to confirm this restoration.

In other words, true forgiveness seeks the best for those who offend or sin against us. Even when they continue to harm us, we should wish them well, as Saint Paul illustrates in Romans 12:14-21.

In Genesis chapters 40-45, Joseph gives us a wonderful example of forgiveness. His brothers sold him into slavery. They did not want to see him again, in fact, they wanted him dead. Joseph was sold as a slave and taken to Egypt.

Later Joseph became a powerful person in Egypt. When famine came upon the land, he was in charge of distributing food to the people who were suffering from hunger. Soon his brothers also came to him looking for food. Here Joseph had a chance for revenge, by refusing to give them food, but instead he forgave his brothers. He chose to repay evil with kindness. He not only forgave them, but gave them what they were searching for and welcomed them once again into a relationship with him. In this way, the family was reunited and became one community. He did not keep them at a distance, but came near them, and their family was restored.

A Forgiveness that Aims at the Conversion of Others

When we forgive, we should also take the responsibility of helping those we forgive to become better people.

The person who goes astray may not be able to find his way back on his own. His way of perceiving things may have become distorted. This person may need assistance from someone to come back to the right path. However, we can only help if we make an effort to build a relationship with that person, instead of keeping him at arm's length.

Many people can only begin in the most minimal way to know their way back when they are offered love and compassion. This love gives them hope that their way to the right path is possible. Where love is strong, even the gates of hell shall not prevail against it. In forgiving others, we must be willing also to become agents of redemption for them.

When God forgave us, He did not leave us to struggle on our own; He came to live among us to help us in our efforts toward perfection. He also sent the Holy Spirit to continue to help us to become better people.

In the parable of the prodigal son, the father not only forgave the son, but he also made an effort to clean him up:

> "But the father ordered his servants, 'Quickly bring the finest robe and put it on him; put a ring on his finger and sandals on his feet.'" (Luke 15:22)

The father didn't want to see his son in dirty and foul-smelling clothes. When we forgive others, let us also help them to clean themselves up. We have a responsibility to help them to become clean again and live a better life. We must pray for them always.

> "But I say to you, love your enemies, and pray for those who persecute you." (Matthew 5:44)

Some Consequences Of Unforgiveness

When we refuse to forgive, there are consequences we have to face. These consequences make us even more vulnerable.

We Become the Devil's Workshop

When we refuse to forgive, we give the devil a chance to open up his workshop in our lives. He will use this space to try to injure our lives and the lives of other people. He will use our lives as a breeding ground for bitterness, hate, revenge, self-pity, calumny, and other things.

Unforgiveness is one of Satan's devices—an instrument, a weapon, a plot, a tool that he uses to destroy us. Unforgiveness in our heart can give Satan a chance to control us by taking away our joy, peace, love and harmony. There is no way we can have joy and peace in our lives when there is bitterness, resentment and unforgiveness in our lives.

We Fall into the Hands of the Torturers

When we refuse to forgive, we automatically fall into the hands of the torturers. These torturers may be such things as fear, loneliness, depression, frustration, anxiety and self-hatred. All these things cause pain in our lives, and can eventually destroy our physical health. This is a consequence of not forgiving.

In the Gospel of Matthew, chapter 18, the servant who failed to forgive was summoned by his master, who said,

> "'You wicked servant! I forgave you your entire debt because you begged me to. Should you not have had pity on your fellow servant, as I had pity on you?' Then in anger his master handed him over to the torturers until he should pay back the whole debt. So will my heavenly Father do to you, unless each of you forgives his brother from his heart."
> (Matthew 18:32-35)

In other words, if we do not want to destroy ourselves, we must learn to forgive others.

No Forgiveness for Us

When we refuse to forgive others, we cut ourselves off from God's forgiveness in our lives. In the gospels, Jesus makes this point clear:

> "If you forgive others their transgressions, your Heavenly Father will forgive you. But if you do not forgive others, neither will your Father forgive your transgressions."
>
> (Matthew 6:14-15)

> "When you stand to pray, forgive anyone against whom you have a grievance, so that your Heavenly Father may in turn forgive you your transgressions." (Mark 11:25-26)

In the book of Sirach, we see the same thing:

> The vengeful will suffer the Lord's vengeance, for He remembers their sins in detail. Forgive your neighbor's injustice; then when you pray, your own sins will be forgiven. Should a man nourish anger against his fellows and expect healing from the Lord? Should a man refuse mercy to his fellows, yet seek pardon for his own sins?
>
> (Sirach 28:1-5)

We Destroy our Relationship with God

When we refuse to forgive, we separate ourselves from God. Unforgiveness ruins our relationship with God and therefore stunts our spiritual growth. We sin when we refuse to forgive.

Unforgiveness interferes with the effectiveness of our prayer life. God is more pleased with prayers offered with a heart full of forgiveness. That is why He tells us to first reconcile with our brother before we bring our sacrifice to the altar. God may put our blessings on hold, until we forgive others. God wants prayers offered *in* love and *with* love.

> "Therefore, if you bring your gift to the altar, and there recall that your brother has anything against you, leave your gift there at the altar, go first and be reconciled with your brother, and then come and offer your gift." (Matthew 5:23-24)

If our relationship with God is destroyed, we will live an unhappy life. True happiness lies in being in communion with our God. God is the source of happiness, so we will never be truly happy if we promote any type of unforgiveness in our lives.

Conclusion

In this book we have discussed some of the saints who practiced this virtue of forgiving one another. Although forgiveness is not easy, it is not impossible. The saints managed to forgive their enemies; we can do it too. However, it is important to realize that we cannot do it alone; we need God's help.

When Jesus told His disciples that they should forgive always, the disciples responded by asking Jesus to increase their faith:

> 4 "And if he wrongs you seven times in one day and returns to you seven times saying, 'I am sorry,' you should forgive him." 5 And the apostles said to the Lord, "Increase our faith." (Luke 17:4-5)

The disciples realized that they needed more *faith* to be able to forgive one another without any limitations. We too must ask Our Lord to increase our faith, so we may forgive.

 **About Leonine Publishers**

Leonine Publishers LLC makes fine Catholic literature available to Catholics throughout the English-speaking world. Leonine Publishers offers an innovative "hybrid" approach to book publication that helps authors as well as readers. Please visit our web site at www.leoninepublishers.com to learn more about us. Browse our online bookstore to find more solid Catholic titles to uplift, challenge, and inspire.

Our patron and namesake is Pope Leo XIII, a prudent, yet uncompromising pope during the stormy years at the close of the 19th century. Please join us as we ask his intercession for our family of readers and authors.

Do you have a book inside you? Visit our web site today. Leonine Publishers accepts manuscripts from Catholic authors like you. If your book is selected for publication, you will have an active part in the production process. This spiritual book is an example of our growing selection of literature for the busy Catholic reader of the 21st century.

www.leoninepublishers.com

www.ingramcontent.com/pod-product-compliance
Lightning Source LLC
Chambersburg PA
CBHW031456040426
42444CB00007B/1125